The Urbana Free Library

To renew materials call
217-367-4057

SCHOLASTIC
News
Nonfiction Readers

Wild
Weather Days

by Katie Marsico

Children's Press®
A Division of Scholastic Inc.
New York Toronto London Auckland Sydney
Mexico City New Delhi Hong Kong
Danbury, Connecticut

These content vocabulary word builders are for grades 1–2.
Consultants: Robert Van Winkle, Chief Meteorologist, WBBH, Fort Myers, Florida; and Jack Williams, Public Outreach Coordinator, American Meteorological Society, Boston, Massachusetts

Reading Consultant: Cecilia Minden-Cupp, PhD, Former Director of the Language and Literacy Program, Harvard Graduate School of Education, Cambridge, Massachusetts

Photographs © 2007: Airphoto-Jim Wark: 21 center; Corbis Images: 23 top left (Tony Demin), back cover, 2, 4 bottom left, 15 (Warren Faidley), 5 bottom right, 13 (Frithjof Hirdes/zefa), 5 top left, 6 (Louie Psihoyos), 5 top right, 5 bottom left, 7, 10, 11 (Jim Reed), 9, 23 bottom left (Mike Theiss/Jim Reed Photography), cover (A & J Verkaik), 23 bottom right (Michael S. Yamashita), 4 top, 17 (David Jay Zimmerman), 4 bottom right, 16 (Jim Zuckerman); Dembinsky Photo Assoc./Victor Pasko/PSU: 20; Graeme Hird/Scene by Hird: 21 bottom; Index Stock Imagery: 1, 19 (Bill Bachmann), 23 top right (DesignPics Inc.); Nature Picture Library Ltd./Aflo: 21 top.

Book Design: Simonsays Design!
Book Production: The Design Lab

Library of Congress Cataloging-in-Publication Data

Marsico, Katie, 1980–
   Wild weather days / Katie Marsico.
      p. cm. — (Scholastic news nonfiction readers)
   Includes bibliographical references and index.
   ISBN-10: 0-531-16771-2
   ISBN-13: 978-0-531-16771-7
   1. Meteorology—Juvenile literature. 2. Weather—Juvenile literature.
I. Title. II. Series.
   QC863.5.T78 2007
   551.55—dc22   2006013308

CONTENTS

Word Hunt 4–5

A Wild Sky 6–7

Thunder and Lightning 8–9

Hail 10–11

Wind 12–13

Hurricanes 14–15

Blizzards 16–17

Wild Weather and You 18–19

**What Else Can You Do on a
 Wild Weather Day?** 20–21

Your New Words 22

**Four Things You Might See
 on a Wild Weather Day** 23

Index 24

Find Out More 24

Meet the Author 24

WORD HUNT

Look for these words as you read. They will be in **bold**.

blizzard
(**bliz**-urd)

hurricane
(**hur**-uh-kane)

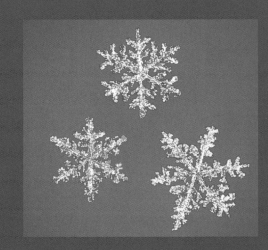

snowflakes
(**snoh**-flayks)

clouds
(kloudz)

hail
(hayl)

thunderstorm
(**thuhn**-dur-storm)

wind
(wind)

A Wild Sky

What's that rumbling over your roof? Do you see those dark **clouds**? We're in for a **thunderstorm**!

Stay inside where it's warm and cozy. There will be some wild weather today!

clouds

Thunderstorms usually occur in spring or summer.

Thunderstorms happen when ice and water rub together inside a cloud.

First, you may see a flash of lightning. Then you'll hear the crackle of thunder.

Some lightning touches the ground.

Hail sometimes falls during thunderstorms. Hail is lumps of ice.

Hail may be as small as a pea or as large as a softball.

hail

Hail comes in all shapes and sizes.

Wind can make wild weather, too! Wind is air that is moving.

Sometimes wind simply shakes colorful leaves from the trees. Other times, powerful storms called tornados happen over land. Tornados are filled with very strong winds.

**The ground is covered with leaves!
It must be a windy autumn day.**

A **hurricane** is another windy storm.

Hurricanes form over warm ocean water. They usually occur during the summer.

Hurricanes stir up heavy wind and rain.

When the weather gets cold, do you enjoy watching the **snowflakes** fall?

Sometimes the wind blows snowflakes sideways. This causes a storm called a **blizzard**.

snowflakes

It's hard to see during a blizzard! Snowflakes blow through the air!

Wild weather is amazing!

It can also be a lot of fun. Have you ever flown a kite when it's super windy? A blizzard's the perfect chance to study snowflakes! And there's nothing cozier than staying inside and listening to the thunder rumble.

What do you like to do best on wild weather days?

WHAT ELSE CAN YOU DO ON A WILD WEATHER DAY?

You can study different types of lightning!

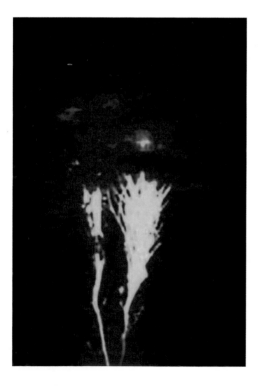

Blue jets appear as very bright flashes of color.

Forked lightning appears as crooked lines that seem to have many branches.

Heat lightning appears as distant, weak flashes of light and usually occurs on hot summer nights. Heat lightning can mean a thunderstorm is on its way.

Sheet lightning appears as large flashes and seems to light up the clouds.

YOUR NEW WORDS

blizzard (**bliz**-urd) a heavy snowstorm

clouds (kloudz) white or gray masses that float in the sky and are made up of water and ice

hail (hayl) small lumps of ice that fall from the sky

hurricane (**hur**-uh-kane) a storm with heavy winds and rain that forms over warm ocean water

snowflakes (**snoh**-flayks) single pieces, or flakes, of snow

thunderstorm (**thuhn**-dur-storm) a storm that happens when ice and water rub together inside a cloud

wind (wind) air that is moving

FOUR THINGS YOU MIGHT SEE ON A WILD WEATHER DAY

rain

snowman

waves

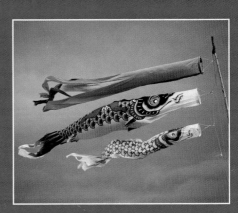

wind socks

INDEX

blizzard, 4, 16, 17, 18

cloud, 5, 6, 8

hail, 5, 10, 11
hurricane, 4, 14, 15

ice, 8, 10

kite, 18

leaves, 12, 13
lightning, 8, 9

oceans, 14

snowflakes, 4, 16, 17, 18
summer, 7, 14

thunder, 8, 18

thunderstorm, 5, 6, 7, 8, 10
tornados, 12
trees, 12

water, 8, 14
wind, 5, 12, 13, 14, 15, 16, 18

FIND OUT MORE

Book:

Chambers, Catherine. *Thunderstorm*. Chicago: Heinemann Library, 2002.

Web site:

Chris Kridler's Sky Diary
http://skydiary.com/kids/

MEET THE AUTHOR:

Katie Marsico is a freelance writer and editor who lives with her family in Chicago, Illinois. Katie enjoys spending time inside with her daughter when the thunder rumbles outside her home.